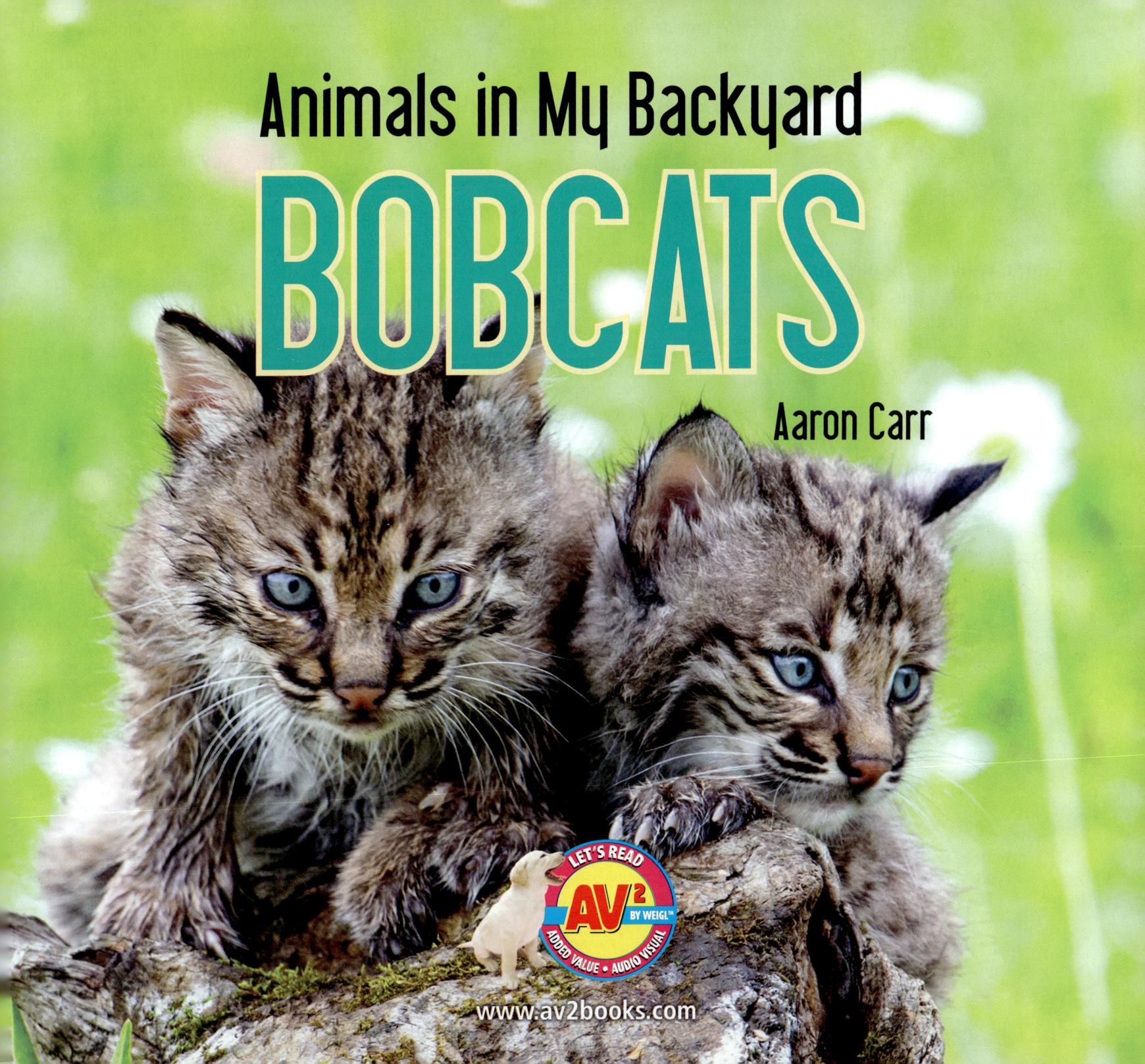

Animals in My Backyard

BOBCATS

Aaron Carr

www.av2books.com

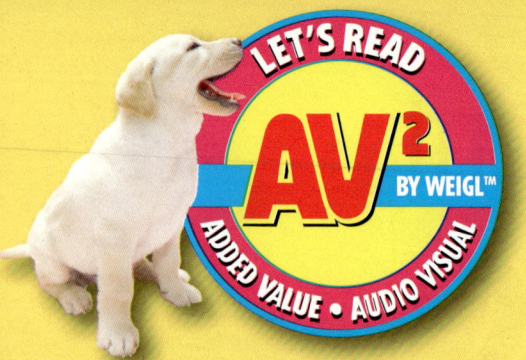

LET'S READ AV²

BY WEIGL™

ADDED VALUE • AUDIO VISUAL

Go to **www.av2books.com**, and enter this book's unique code.

BOOK CODE

K879982

AV² by Weigl brings you media enhanced books that support active learning.

AV² provides enriched content that supplements and complements this book. Weigl's AV² books strive to create inspired learning and engage young minds in a total learning experience.

Your AV² Media Enhanced books come alive with...

Audio
Listen to sections of the book read aloud.

Video
Watch informative video clips.

Embedded Weblinks
Gain additional information for research.

Try This!
Complete activities and hands-on experiments.

Key Words
Study vocabulary, and complete a matching word activity.

Quizzes
Test your knowledge.

Slide Show
View images and captions, and prepare a presentation.

... and much, much more!

Published by AV² by Weigl
350 5th Avenue, 59th Floor New York, NY 10118
Websites: www.av2books.com   www.weigl.com

Library of Congress Cataloging-in-Publication Data
Carr, Aaron.
 Bobcats / Aaron Carr.
     pages cm -- (Animals in my backyard)
 Includes index.
 ISBN 978-1-4896-2938-8 (hard cover : alk. paper) -- ISBN 978-1-4896-2939-5 (soft cover : alk. paper) -- ISBN 978-1-4896-2940-1 (single user ebook)--
ISBN 978-1-4896-2941-8 (multi-user ebook)
 1. Bobcat--Juvenile literature. I. Title.
 QL737.C23C354 2014
 599.75'36--dc23
                              2014039094

Printed in the United States of America in Brainerd, Minnesota
1 2 3 4 5 6 7 8 9 0 18 17 16 15 14

122014
WEP051214

Project Coordinator: Heather Kissock   Designer: Mandy Christiansen

Weigl acknowledges Getty Images, Alamy, Minden Pictures, and iStock as the primary image suppliers for this title.

2

Animals in My Backyard
BOBCATS

CONTENTS

Meet the bobcat.

He is a big cat with a short tail.

He lives with his mother when he is young.

When he is young, his mother teaches him how to hunt.

He can run fast with his long legs.

With his long legs, he can jump higher than a basketball net.

He climbs trees with his long, sharp claws.

His long, sharp claws
help him catch his food.

He has a coat of brown fur with spots.

Brown fur with spots helps
him hide in grass and bushes.

He hunts by using his keen hearing and sight.

His keen hearing and sight help him track animals from far away.

He makes homes in caves and tree stumps.

Caves and tree stumps give him safe places to sleep.

He lives in North America.

In North America, he can be found in forests and deserts.

If you meet the bobcat,
he may be surprised.
He might run away.

If you meet the bobcat,
stay away.

BOBCAT FACTS

These pages provide more detail about the interesting facts found in the book. They are intended to be used by adults as a learning support to help young readers round out their knowledge of each animal featured in the *Animals in My Backyard* series.

Pages 4–5

Bobcats are big cats with short tails. The bobcat is named for its short tail, which looks like it has been cut short, or "bobbed." The tail is about 4 to 8 inches (10 to 20 centimeters) long. Bobcats can be more than 3 feet (1 meter) long and stand up to 2 feet (0.6 m) tall. Males can weigh up to 30 pounds (13.6 kilograms), while females can weigh as much as 20 pounds (9 kg).

Pages 6–7

Bobcats live with their mother when they are young. Bobcats give birth to between one and six kittens at a time. Kittens drink their mother's milk for the first two months before they start to eat solid food. By five months of age, kittens begin to learn how to hunt with their mother. They stay with their mother for up to 12 months before going off to live on their own.

Pages 8–9

Bobcats have long legs. Their long legs and large paws give bobcats great speed, acceleration, and leaping ability. Bobcats can jump up to 12 feet (3.7 m) high. They can cover a distance of 10 feet (3 m) in a single leap. They can reach speeds of more than 30 miles (48 kilometers) per hour over short distances.

Pages 10–11

Bobcats have long, sharp claws. These curved claws can measure up to 0.75 inches (1.9 cm) long. Bobcats have five toes on their front paws and four toes on their hind paws. Like most cats, the bobcat's claws are retractable. Bobcats keep their claws retracted when walking, so they are not visible in their tracks. They use their claws for climbing, catching prey, and defending themselves from predators.

Bobcats have brown fur with dark and light patches. A bobcat's coat of brown fur may have a red, tawny, or gray tinge with interspersed spots. The colors are darker along the back and fade to lighter shades on the underside. The coat blends in well with the vegetation found in the bobcat's habitat. This built-in camouflage helps the bobcat to stay out of sight.

Bobcats use their excellent hearing and sight to hunt their prey. These senses are used to track and stalk prey such as rabbits, birds, and rodents. Bobcats also rely on their camouflage to ambush prey. They hide in vegetation and pounce on prey when it comes close. Bobcats do most of their hunting around dusk and dawn.

Bobcats make use of several dens. They typically have one main den and several secondary dens. The main den is usually in a cave. Other den sites include fallen trees and brush piles. The dens provide protection and shelter while the bobcat sleeps. Bobcats spread their dens throughout their home ranges, which cover about 25 to 30 square miles (65 to 78 square kilometers).

Bobcats live in North America. They range from southern Canada to southern Mexico. Bobcats are comfortable in a wide range of habitats, including forests, deserts, swamps, mountains, chaparrals, and even suburban areas. However, they prefer areas with diverse landscapes, such as areas where woodlands and grasslands meet.

If you meet a bobcat, stay back. Although bobcats rarely attack humans, people should still exercise caution when encountering these cats. In rare cases, a bobcat may have a disease called rabies, which may make it more likely to attack. People should keep their distance and make loud noises to scare the bobcat away.

KEY WORDS

Research has shown that as much as 65 percent of all written material published in English is made up of 300 words. These 300 words cannot be taught using pictures or learned by sounding them out. They must be recognized by sight. This book contains 40 common sight words to help young readers improve their reading fluency and comprehension. This book also teaches young readers several important content words. These words are paired with pictures to aid in learning and improve understanding.

Page	Sight Words First Appearance
4	the
5	a, big, he, is, with
6	him, his, how, lives, mother, to, when, young
8	can, long, run
9	than
10	trees
11	food, help
12	has, of
13	and, in
14	by
15	animals, away, far, from
16	give, homes, makes, places
19	be, found
20	if, may, might, you

Page	Content Words First Appearance
4	bobcat
5	cat, tail
8	legs
9	basketball net
10	claws
12	coat, fur, spots
13	bushes, grass
14	hearing, sight
16	caves, stumps
18	North America
19	deserts, forests